WHAT'S IT ALL ABOUT?

by

"Anyman"

authorHOUSE®

AuthorHouse™
1663 Liberty Drive
Bloomington, IN 47403
www.authorhouse.com
Phone: 1-800-839-8640

First published by AuthorHouse 2/25/2011

ISBN: 978-1-4567-2963-9 (e)
ISBN: 978-1-4567-2962-2 (sc)

Printed in the United States of America

Any people depicted in stock imagery provided by Thinkstock are models,
and such images are being used for illustrative purposes only.
Certain stock imagery © Thinkstock.

This book is printed on acid-free paper.

CONTENTS

PART III

PART IV

SOMETHING ABOUT THE BOOK

There are 48 writings divided into four parts. Most are conversations between a father and son.

There are conversations about religion–defined as the relationship between a person and the Creator.

There are conversations about morals. There are conversations just for fun.

And, Part II, a few guest authors who never wrote before but will contribute stories made up out of Song Titles.

Because music and all of the above are a part of–Life.

NOTE: Eight of the conversations between father and son are Roman Catholic–that is part of their Life–Because–that's what they are.

Series Dedication

This Series must be dedicated to Anybody. To the person who would hold onto the moment from the past–the fond memory–the guilt. That they may enjoy the moment of the present. That they may have Hope for the future. No anxiety. *Peace of Mind*!

And also, a special dedication to Kelly–the girl who suffered much–she asked for health that she might enjoy all things–she was given peace–that she might enjoy life!

Special thanks to Bob, my typists and to all the authors in Part II, including my children and others. They wrote great stories starting from nothing and their reward will be the same!

Oh, and let's not forget ALFIE–*Anychild*–with hopes for all to be–and thanks to all who are–*Like a Child*!

Part I

THE ALPHA, ALFIE

One early Sunday morning while sitting at Mass, with the wind whistling outside and a baby beginning to cry, the priest posed a question to think about during the week–WHAT ARE YOU LOOKING FOR? He gave us the answer–happiness. Then why should we have to think all week? But in the dull days of winter, after football and before baseball, it couldn't hurt–could it? But how do you think? To give us such a chore could ruin our stream of consciousness or our stream of actions which are giving us happiness anyway, aren't they? But why not try, Alfie.

Father is right, we are looking for happiness, but why can't we find it with our own intellect and will? Could it be because of what we choose? Maybe we need to ask the Supreme Intellect and Will, the person we call God, how to find happiness. What does He say? Of course, keep My Commandments, love one another! Maybe we have been looking for 'instant happiness' and happiness really begins with peace of mind from keeping the Commandments and then loving others and even loving God instead of fear! If we look about us, we see people who are happy and have been happy for years. WHY ARE THEY HAPPY? Because they do the above and have a different attitude toward God, namely, complete Trust in Him! Let His Intellect and Will control things. Let prayer control my thinking and will–(is what they do).

But how do we change our attitude toward God, Alfie?

Maybe if we recognize that *He is a person who loves us*, we can recognize His attitude toward us. Could it be that:

1. He is not waiting to point out our past mistakes?
2. He is not out to get us?
3. He wants us to smile?
4. He is pleased when we laugh?

Does this mean he actually wants us to enjoy life? Didn't He create us to be sad? Well, Alfie, maybe it is time to look at things differently. *THE ONLY THING THAT BECOMES REALLY IMPORTANT IS THE IMMEDIATE EVENT BEFORE US*. As long as the next thing we do is not a choice of wrong or a thought of anxiety or some other useless pondering, we might really begin to enjoy things–the pool game, the Mass, the song, the laughter, the prayer (even the Rosary), the Bingo game, changing the diaper, the sunset, the Broadway show, the homerun, the conversation and even accepting the pain! And if we persist in meeting only the event before us, till death, we need not fear that moment, we need not panic, lest we miss finishing the pool game. And finally, (WAKE UP, ALFIE)–

We must realize that we are not competing with anybody, we must do the best we can and be content if others appear to be doing better. When we arrive at the correct 'State of Mind', we can even use the word happy rather than content with what others are accomplishing. We are all on the same team.

We must proceed with confidence and as it takes years to be come a mature adult, maybe, someday, if we persist, we will be come a child! So Alfie, if we are looking for happiness, we look to the person who wants us to have it more than we do! And how do we begin–Alpha?

We begin by–OUR FATHER..........THY WILL BE DONE..........

4

WHAT TIME IS IT, ALFIE?

We forgot to change the clock. Do we set it an hour ahead or an hour behind? Alfie and I were both thinking, looking at the clock. The ticking seemed to cut the silence and the second hand kept moving, counting the minutes as it had done for so many years.

I wonder whatever happened to Brother Paulus, I thought? I'll never forget what he told us about the clock.

Imagine an empty room. An experiment. The clock is taken apart, piece by piece and scattered in every corner. The room is sealed. Several months go by and we return. The clock is sitting in the middle of the room ticking the correct time! How could this be? Let's consider all the possibilities we can think of. Chance, some kind of luck or unknown cause of this event. How about mice, or even ants who gathered all the pieces together and presto–or how about that storm we had–the pieces were blown together and combined with the heat in the room and the position of the moon–presto. We may never know the answer, because everybody has an idea. I got it, I think I heard somebody say, spontaneous combustion–that sounds good–make up anything and give it the old scientific jazz–any intellectual scientist can come up with something brilliant and explain it in profound terms, however, they need more study–it is still a mystery–a what?

But wait, Brother Paulus has an idea. He thinks that somehow, a watchmaker got into the room. Using his intellect and will, the watchmaker collected all the intricate parts of the clock, put them together and sat the clock in the middle of the room. Is he kidding? Nobody will buy that—it makes too much sense and besides it is too simple.

Brother Paulus changed the topic—or did he? Look at the sun, he said—the moon, the stars, a tree, a flower, the animals, the planets—a baby—look at the intricate parts of all these things! They are more complicated than a clock! As it takes an intellect and a will—the person of the watchmaker—to put a clock together—so too—it took a Supreme Intellect and will—the *PERSON* we call God—to put the Universe together!

But this also makes too much sense. Boy, could the intellectuals tear that argument apart. All they have to say is something about cosmic rays with such energy force (or whatever they say), that somehow, whatever it is, some type of super matter, produces a non-material intellect and a non-material will. Whatever happened to—*you can't give what you don't have*? And if this super matter does have intellect and will to give—what are they going to call it? Make the truth fit your Subjective demand. Let any scientist explain it to you—the label scientist demands that we listen to the authority! Frankly, Scarlet!

And I am tired of the scientist and all those who don't do any thinking, scoffing at the Christian who says some things are a mystery. We are not blind faith! We combine faith and reason. Try it sometime! It's called true logic!

They can have their mysteries and I can have mine—but one of mine is not how the Universe got started. I'll take Brother Paulus and the logic of the clock anyday, even though the Person in control has some necessary rules. You don't have to worry about any rules of the Creator with any scientific belief or denial—or do you? Belief? How can any scientist (not all) criticize a man of faith—and have faith in their own belief? It is so easy for the scientist—who gets all the respect—to say to the man of faith—where is your proof? Well, it is just as easy for the man of Faith to say—where is your proof? His answer—we have a theory that we are fairly certain of but we need more time than the thousands of years we had—it is still something we can't fully understand and explain (in other words—a mystery). Tell em again, Brother Paulus. Am I being redundant? Well, Frankly Scarlet!

THE BOOK, has all the answers. It can say something quick without getting mad. I wish I could.

Someplace in *THE BOOK*, it says—in essence—Scientists in their analysis and review of the product—miss the Author!

Alfie was yelling the correct time from upstairs. I hadn't noticed him leaving the room. What time is it, Alfie?

LOVING PEOPLE, ALFIE

It was Sunday morning, and Alfie and I were not going to Church. For the first time, we went on Saturday night. Where is that paper boy? He always sleeps late on Sunday. Alfie came down the stairs and turned on the radio. It was my favorite singer. I went in the kitchen. Scrambled or over light, Alfie? Just toast came the reply? What a voice–not yours Alfie–but George Burns. The song doesn't make sense, Alfie said. I hadn't been listening to the words–"Using things and loving people is the way its got to be for loving things and using people just brings misery"–is what he was singing.

No Alfie, I said–when I heard the words–once you really hear them, they make a lot of sense. Just think of some things we use. We use money to buy what we want, we use drink to enjoy a party, we use a car to get where we are going, and we could go on and on. But if we are in love with the money–if we are in love with the drink–if we are in love with the car–we will not be happy and will not know why. Loving things never brings happiness, especially if we use people to get the things.

All of a sudden, George Burns sounded even better. Turn it up, Alfie, I said. His voice faded into the commercial–Loving people is the Way...

YOU WIN AGAIN, ALFIE

T.V. is boring again. I got an idea, Alfie. I just bought a new Dictionary today. Let's open to a page at random, pick the first word we see, read the definition and then each give their opinion as to how the word relates to Life.

Remember that day, Alfie? I saved the first five words and wrote down the answers we gave. I can't believe we didn't cheat. The first word at random was–trawl–wouldn't ya know I said–a word we never heard of.

1. *Trawl*–a large net dragged along the bottom of a fishing bank.

I went for the obvious, the Apostles, fishers of men. But I liked your answer–the best way to catch Charlie Tuna.

2. *Leash*–a cord, strap etc. by which a dog or the like is held in check.

Your answer related to your walks with our dog, Crystal, and you were right, she carries her own leash so there are exceptions to this definition. Again, I went for the obvious and said it was something your mother thinks she has on me or is it something she does and I think she doesn't or something you kids think you have on both of us but you don't, at least we think you don't but maybe you do? Well, anyway–let's go to the next word.

3. *Engage*–to pledge (oneself), to bind by a promise of marriage.

I immediately had to look up the definition of pledge– the condition of being given or held as security for a contract,

9

payment etc. This I understood–payment–and–held–back to leash again. So I said, down payment on the purchase of a leash. You went for the obvious on this one–your sisters getting engaged.

4. *Masculine*–Male, of men or boys–suitable to or having qualities regarded as characteristic of men; strong, vigorous, manly etc. (Yea!) Boy, am I glad we didn't get that other word. I presume it's in the dictionary since Webster can define any thing.

Your answer as to how it related to life was–Jim Rice, of the Boston Red Sox. I went for a joke since the other kind thinks that's what we are–"How many chauvinistic pigs does it take to clean a toilet? None, it's a woman's job!" (just kidding girls). Boy, am I glad Mommie wasn't in on that game, Alfie!

5. *Step*–a single movement of the foot, as in walking, the distance covered by such movement, a short distance, a rest for the foot in climbing, as a stair.

Your answer was the step unto the moon by the astronaut–"One small step for man, one giant leap for mankind."

This was the best answer but I remember, at the time, going into a discourse on taking life one step at a time since it is a short distance to heaven and everything is passing with each step!

I went on and on and then I remember saying, Wake up! You win again, Alfie.

WHY NOT MARRIAGE, ALFIE?

Alfie was only eleven years old and his friend's sister was getting married. The couple had lived together for several years and decided to have a church wedding as their parents had always wanted. Alfie and his friends were talking in the living room as I was about to come downstairs. He knows more than I thought he knew! Could he really have remembered what I said to him at five days old when I held him in my arms? I told him all about "IT" then–just to get it over with. Maybe that Doctor is right–everything is retained in the subconscious. But wait a minute–as I continued to listen–that ain't the way I told him!

That evening, as we were about to play a game of chess, Alfie asked me why people had to get married. It was then that I told him I had overheard his friends talking about pleasure alone.

There is nothing wrong with pleasure, Alfie. When God created us, He made us the way we are and saw that it was good. But He never meant pleasure alone.

Once there were three sisters living in the country. Their names were plus, minus and zero. They never heard of and, therefore, never wore shoes. The big day was here–plus and minus were going to the city–zero was too young. Minus found out about shoes from a group of girls who wore the right shoe on the left foot and the left shoe on the right foot. Plus also found out about shoes but from girls who wore the right shoe on the right foot and the left shoe on the left foot.

Back at home, minus was very proud and wore her new shoes all the time, never admitting how they hurt. She bragged and showed zero.

One day, zero took the shoes of plus and plus watched as she stumbled and stumbled. Let me show you, plus said. Once zero had put the right shoe on the right foot and the left shoe on the left foot, she walked with ease, the way the shoemaker intended.

I am talking about–if the word will come out–SEX– there, I said it Alfie!

Zero = the person who knows nothing about Sex.

Minus = the person who thinks Sex is pleasure alone.

Plus = the person who learned about marriage–love and pleasure.

You see, Alfie, just as the shoemaker intended the right shoe for the right foot and the left shoe for the left foot–so, the Creator intended parents to have love and pleasure–to share in creation and continue the human race. But can't you have love and pleasure without marriage, Alfie asked? Of course you can, I replied. But in marriage you are taking a vow before God and asking His help to keep your relationship strong and not overcome by selfishness. So–why not marriage, Alfie?

I WONDER WHERE RAY IS, ALFIE?

Years ago, Alfie, when we were in the seventh grade, I think it was Sister Louise or Sister Eileen, well anyway, I am not making this up—Some Sister told us a story and the essence of it was—or still is—the same man who was chosen to play Christ, years later, was chosen to play Pilate in the same play.

Well, guess what, Alfie. Years ago, approximately thirty-six, in college, I was chosen to play Christ. Where are you, Ray Howard? I can play Pilate!

It is an eerie feeling to think of that. Did you make that story up, Sister? It is also an eerie feeling to play Christ.

Now, I will tell the rest of the story, Ray, as Paul Harvey would say.

How did you ever get me to do that, Ray? You had a way with words. I was scared stiff—but guess what—they talk about the Hail Mary pass, well it works. I was shaking before the play began. I said a Hail Mary—and a complete calm came over me! I figure Mary didn't want to embarrass her son. But I'm not too sure of that—you remember—I tripped in the Garden scene. But it didn't bother me—I wish I had that calm all my life—but I was Christ for only an hour. I was pretty good though—remember, you told me—and you know all about acting and make—up—they even said I looked like Christ.

Acting? I wasn't acting—at least not on the Cross—you had me standing on one bare foot (with the other on top)

13

on that extension ladder. Try it for fifteen minutes! I was in pain and thought I would fall before the scene was over. Frank had a good spot behind me singing the words I was mouthing–too slow! I couldn't wait to die. And everybody said what a great job I did. You could have picked anybody to stand on that ladder–the pain shown on my face was real!

Thank you, Christ, for what you did. A real cross, nails, vinegar, three hours! And there are still a lot of people who know not what they do!

Did you ever make any more plays, Ray? Would you like to do that one again? Need a Pilate? Go ahead and ask me–ask Anyman–How does it sound–I wash my hands of the whole thing!

How about you, Alfie? Would you do it? You could! I wonder where Ray is, Alfie?

THINKING

One Sunday night while Alfie was on Christmas vacation, we turned off the T.V. and began to play Alfie's favorite thinking game. He liked to think of people nobody heard of and imagine them to be the stars of history. For example, he pictured our postman as Paul Revere giving the warning–the bills are coming, the bills are coming! And the fat lady in the circus as Mary Poppins–flying close to the ground.

But that night, since it was close to Christmas, Alfie asked who we could get to play Santa Claus. He immediately thought of Christ because of all the good he does for people. Alfie said we could take the X out of Xmas and say Santa X is coming or X Claus is coming. No, I said, that would confuse the children.

You see, a long time ago, many people got Santa Claus to play Christ. But saying Merry Clausman or Merry Santamas was too hard so they used an X. Someday, maybe people who must use an X will at least say Merry Christ X.

Christ so loved children that He would never want them to lose Santa Claus. People fail to see that we need them both!

Well, Alfie, I think it is time for sleep. Sleep in peace, Alfie, Heavenly Peace. Remember, Santa Claus is coming, so–Merry Christmas!

SPEAKS FOR ITSELF, ALFIE

After we finished playing the dictionary game the other night, Alfie, and you went to bed, I decided to do the same thing with the Bible and I wrote down the first thing I saw when I opened the book. I chose the section and then opened at random to a page in that section and here is the result:

(NOTE: Two picked from Wisdom and two picked from Ecclesiasticus.)

Proverbs–Let not thy heart envy sinners: but be thou in the fear of the Lord all the day long.

Wisdom–But all men are vain, in whom there is not the knowledge of God: and who by these good things that are seen, could not understand him that is, neither by attending to the works have acknowledged who was the workman.

Wisdom–For the hope of the wicked is as dust, which is blown away with the wind, and as a thin froth which is dispersed by the storm: and a smoke that is scattered abroad by the wind: and as the remembrance of a guest of one day that passeth by.

Ecclesiasticus–Much experience is the crown of old men, and fear of God is their glory.

Ecclesiasticus –Ye that fear the Lord, wait for his mercy: and go not aside from him, lest ye fail. Ye that fear the Lord, believe and your reward shall not be made void. Ye that fear the Lord, hope in him: and mercy shall come to you for your delight. Ye that fear the Lord, love him, and your hearts shall be enlightened.

My children behold the generations of men: and know ye that no one hath hoped in the Lord, and hath been confounded. For who hath continued in his commandment, and hath been forsaken? Or who hath called upon him, and he despised him?

For God is Compassionate and merciful, and will forgive sins in the day of tribulation: and he is a protector to all that seek him in truth.

Matthew–And answering the king will say to them, 'Amen I say to you, as long as you did it for one of these, the least of my brethren, you did it for me.'

Mark–And the Pharisees came forth, and began to dispute with him, demanding from him a sign from heaven, to test him.

And sighing deeply in spirit, he said, "Why does this generation demand a sign? Amen I say to you, a sign shall not be given to this generation."

Luke–And it was told him, "Thy mother and thy brethren are standing outside, wishing to see thee." But he answered and said to them, "My mother and my brethren are they who hear the word of God, and act upon it."

John–The Chief steward called the bridegroom and said to him, "Every man at first sets forth the good wine, and when they have drunk freely, then that which is poorer. But thou hast kept the good wine until now."

Timothy–Do not lay hands hastily upon anyone, and do not be a partner in other men's sins. Keep thyself chaste.

St. Peter–For it is better, if the will of God should so will, that you suffer for doing good than for doing evil. Because Christ also died for sins, the Just for the unjust, that he might bring us to God. Put to death indeed in the flesh, he was brought to life in the spirit–

St. Paul–we see now through a mirror in an obscure manner, but then face to face. Now I know in part, but then I shall know even as I have been known.

This is what I actually found at random, Alfie. You might ask, how I could be so lucky to find such great words. Well, it doesn't matter what page or section you come to–all the words are great.

So anytime you are feeling 'down', open the Bible to any page at random and listen to the advice–for this great work–Speaks For Itself, Alfie!

AND YOU TOO, ALFIE

T.V. is boring again and I don't feel like playing the dictionary game, Alfie said. Well, let's play another game, Alfie.

Make a list of all your favorite songs and then make a story out of the list. I'll show you how it's done.

First, write down any songs, as they come into your mind.

These are the songs that come into my mind:

Wish I Was Eighteen
Somewhere Over the
    Rainbow
As Time Goes By
Sound of Music
Can't Get Started
Each Time I See A Crowd
    of People
With My Eyes Wide Open
The Wayward Wind
Key Largo
South of the Border
Because of You
Make the World Go Away
You Belong to Me
Winter Wonderland

Heart and Soul
Chicago, My Kind of Town
There Are Such Things
Tree in the Meadow
Imagination
Once Upon a Time
Stormy Weather

Magic Moments
Alfie
Nevertheless
You, You, You

Again
Dream
White Christmas

Easter Parade
Wish Upon A Star
Cattle Call
Rejoice, Rejoice, The
    Angels Sang
Cry
Inkadinkadoo

I Love Life
Perfect World
Once in Awhile
Count Every Star
Sunny Side of the Street
Unforgettable
Someday

And one more to make an *odd* number since this is an *odd* game–There I said it Again. Yes, that's a song, Alfie!

Once upon a time, we were in my kind of town, Chicago, on the sunny side of the street, and there was a *sound of music* which could be heard drifting in with the wayward wind. The Senator was about to give a talk but he couldn't get started with his speech at the Easter Parade because of this sound. I was in charge of the ceremonies and knew I was in for more than stormy weather if I couldn't find where this disturbance was coming from. It sounded like Cattle call coming from over the rainbow. I felt like going to Key Largo or South of the Border because I love life. Boy, I wish I was eighteen again, but, nevertheless, I can't make the world go away and must work because of you, Alfie.

With my eyes wide open, I began the search by the tree in the meadow. Once in awhile, you have to wish upon a star and try your best with all your heart and soul.

Magic Moments! I saw a crowd of people, like a mirage, in a Winter Wonderland, including you, Alfie, but since you belong to me, I knew it wasn't you, you, you and it wouldn't be a White Christmas unless I found that *sound of music*. There, I said it again.

As time goes by, I was about to cry when I finally found the sound–it was Jimmie in the crowd of people, singing, again, Inkadinkadoo and I immediately yelled–Stop The Music!–and the Senator was able to give his speech.

Now you have a new unforgettable game to play, Alfie. Did I leave any song out? Count every star, I mean—count every song—right now—I am sure you will find I used them all.

And remember this Alfie—if you use your imagination in life you will be able to Rejoice, as the Angels sang and help make this a perfect world—someday.

Well, Goodnight Mrs. Kalabash, wherever you are—and you too, Alfie!

NOT ANYMORE TODAY

Do you ever talk to yourself? *Come on*–admit it. So do I. Today is my day—well, so is every day, but I was reminded of something today, my mother. She has been gone a number of years now. One of my assignments for the day was (I can't believe I got it done)–to reach 'knick–knacks' on the mantle and take them down for cleaning–surprising how many things my wife gathered over the years, to make this a better home.

It is an hour and a half before game time and my favorite day and season–Saturday–Fall–and college football. Well, I also like–Saturday–Summer–and the Red Sox. I am glad they don't play in the same season.

Nothing to do but to smoke my cigar and talk to myself. I left one little deer or doe or something on the mantle because it just didn't look right bare.

I am sitting here, looking at two of the pieces–one, a little boy, and one, a little girl–heads lowered–reading a book. (Whoever made these must have lived in a different reality than me).

They belonged to my mother. I saw them often when I was growing up. I never asked her what they meant–but they were very special to her.

Maybe I will read the paper. Enter–my wife again– she thanked me, made a remark about the doe and began dusting the "Shadow Box", as she called it.

Dusting–back to my mother again. I visited her every

day in the hospital toward the end. It was Mother's Day, Sunday, and my mother and I were in her hospital room. She was wearing her new dress and her hair had been done. Enter–in uniform, a cleaner from the hospital. He had a long dust mop and without saying a word–reached and dusted *one side* of the light fixture above and left. My mother and I were both watching him, not saying a word either. When he left the room, we turned and looked at each other–"It looks a lot better now, doesn't it", she said–and we both laughed!

I think I will turn on the T.V. now–I don't feel like talking to myself–Not Anymore Today.

WHY DO GOOD PEOPLE
SUFFER, ALFIE?

Author's note: I prayed for this girl Kelly, and she sent me a thank you note with a cigar–I then wrote this.

Remember when I told you about the Alpha, Alfie. We were talking about happiness, and thinking too much and I said "We can think about suffering and how we would change things"–Well, a very good person asked me why good people have to suffer? And you know what, Alfie, I can't answer that question. It is something we all think about and it bothers us when we don't have the answers. We get upset. When a family is lost and the child asks where they are going, the parent some times gives a quick remark that doesn't answer the question. But why should this question be any different than other questions–how high is up?–how high is the moon?–No–I think somebody did answer that question.

But, long ago, Alfie, there was a very good man and He had a great Father. He knew the answer! However, He still tried to get out of it.

But, Alfie, He knew His Father would not allow anything that wasn't necessary because of how much the Father loved Him. So He accepted what happened and to this day many people have been made happy because of His suffering.

Alfie was listening intently and finally remarked, "you did answer the question!"

No, Alfie, I said. You see, I am not suffering like the good man or the nice young girl who asked the question. Maybe tomorrow I will be. But today, I can't help this girl and I feel like the parent who can't tell the child which way they are going. I only know that many good people have suffered over the years and a lot of these people were Saints, very close to the Father. You mean there is nothing we can do, Alfie asked? Yes, there is, I replied, but we have to go a step further than the good man who said, "Thy will be done." We have to say "Give us this day..."

I will say a prayer for her, Alfie. But first, I think I will have a cigar!

WHY BE SAD, ALFIE?

Alfie came home from school all excited. His teacher who is always sad told them that Humpty Dumpty was pushed! He scrambled but couldn't get up. All the king's men came to help. Turn him over lightly, one screamed. The hard boiled leader wouldn't give up, and they tried to pick him up softly–but the sun was too hot and in the end Humpty was fried. And if you believed all this–the yolk is on you!

Now why can't our teacher tell stories everyday, Alfie asked? She is always so sad.

Well, Alfie, I said. Many good people are sad because they see all the suffering in the world and all the sin–the wrong that is being done. And some good people are very sad when they do wrong themselves. But these people are not sad all the time. And as long as they keep trying–they are happy.

But the saddest people, Alfie, are those who do self–sacrifice in the name of God but really for themselves–they never smile–they never laugh–they are the experts at being sad, and they want everyone to see how good they are and how they are not like other people.

Your teacher is not like that or she couldn't have told that story–she is probably just serious most of the time and there is nothing wrong with that–don't confuse a serious person with a sad person. But even a serious person knows how to smile and laugh.

You may not believe this but it was many years before I found out Humpty Dumpty was an egg—but this does not shatter (pun intended) my belief in a need for Humpty and others like him, including Miss Muffett.

Somewhere over the rainbow, maybe, someday, Alfie, the world will be able to have joy and laugh and rejoice in peace! But till then, pray for this, do your part, smile and laugh along the way (this does not mean you are not concerned). So—why be sad, Alfie?

JUST THINKING

Talking to myself again. I like the early morning. Today, rye toast with peanut–butter. Good cup of coffee. Cigar. I'm in control.

Peanut–butter on toast. I never heard of that till the trip to Montreal. Instead of jelly–little butter things filled with peanut–butter served with toast. I always liked peanut–butter over jelly–why couldn't I figure that out. Maybe we should talk more with Canada–who knows what other ideas they might have? And when we first got there–kinda cold but across the street from the hotel was this girl in a bathing suit, lying on a car–everybody was looking and talking about her–then some guy came and carried her into the store–she, or it was a manikin!

And thinking of coffee–yesterday outside the dough–nut shop–guy says to his friend, "the one without sugar and cream is black"–and he was serious!

People are funny. Which reminds me of Julia at work. I was going from my office to the other end of the building and there was Julia, all excited–"Did you hear?–Roz won $600 in a lottery or something–when is my day going to come? Calm down, Julia–just tell me the month and day *only* when you were born. October 18th, she said quickly. That will be your day! Your birth day! Now, I said, tell me the year, and I will tell you something else about yourself–1934 came the quick reply. Now I will tell you how old you are!

Nobody really knew her age before–and I respect her

right to keep it a secret–I haven't told too many people–only a couple–maybe several!

And thinking of age and the office, what Pat did is equal to Julia. I told her the standard age joke to set somebody up–usually when they're retiring–Mary or whoever, you say, was talking about age the other day and said there were three signs of age: 1) Loss of memory, 2) loss of reflexes–and–she couldn't remember the third. Pat thought that was 'cute' and the next morning, she was having coffee with her husband and age happened to come into the conversation. Pat mentioned we were talking about age and not even telling it as a joke, said–let's see, there are three signs of old age–loss of memory and–her husband about to drink his coffee–spilled it all over, laughing so hard–Pat couldn't remember the second sign!

The last day of the year–everything quiet at work–have to stir something up. We should sing "auld lang syne"–by the way–what does that mean? This got their attention. I laughed to myself–but wait–what does that mean, I thought? All these years and I never knew what I was singing–neither did they as I listened to all the commotion–somebody phoned down stairs–they didn't know either. Finally, Julia phoned the newspaper–"long time since"–was the answer. It doesn't fit. Oh well, it's been *a long time since* Julia got anything straight anyway. Maybe somebody will know New Years Eve–on second thought–maybe I will ask again next Century!

Postscript to this: Two days later, I heard that Julia had 15 people at her house for New Year's dinner. She announced that she had a "trivia' for everybody and asked if anybody knew what "auld lang syne" meant? Julia was beaming as nobody knew. Soon they were all attacking her, for when they asked her what it meant, she drew a blank and couldn't remember!

Resolutions! This year, I am going to resolve–never to wave at anybody on my lunch hour, again–not after my experience with Jim C. For about three years, I have been waving to Jim C., when I would see him, once in a while, and he would wave back–we never passed each other on the same side of the street, so we never got to talk about the good old days in high school when Jim C., Bill L., me, and some other guys would get together and play football. At least, not until this year!

My car was in the garage–and there was Jim C. –Hi Jim, problem with your car? Said Jim–I've been trying to remember who you are? Don't you remember–I said–in disbelief, I used to play football with you and Bill L. when you lived on Western Ave.! My name is Jim, he said, but I never knew any Bill L. and I never lived on Western Ave! Have a nice day, Jim. See you around town!

Good morning, Alfie! You slept late this morning. I was just thinking of some funny things that happened. Which do you think is funnier, a good joke or a real happening?

Let me tell you a joke, Alfie, and then, a real happening and let's see which gets higher on the old laughameter.

First, a joke told on Johnny Carson–Man from back woods of Tennessee, tells old lady he is going to N.Y.C. and she asks him to look up her son and tell him to write–she pleaded–please tell him to write! O.K., he says but N.Y.C. is a pretty big place–what's his name? John Dun, she said.

In N.Y.C., the man is riding along Broadway in a cab and sees a sign–Dun and Bradstreet–stop the cab, he says–goes into the building and asks–Do you have a John here?–Yea, three doors down–he goes three doors down and sees a guy coming out–are you Dun, he says?–the guy looks at him strangely–well yea, he replied–Write your mother!

O.K.–calm down, Alfie–that's enough of a smile–wait until you hear the real happening!

I was away at college–talking to Joe S.–about jokes and the first joke we could remember. Now Joe S., was one of the smartest guys in the class–but he had lived a very sheltered life–and I mean sheltered–he was different–innocent, may be a better word, whatever, but everybody loved Joe S.

I guess the oldest joke, I heard, Joe–was about the Indian who drank so much tea, he went home and drowned in his own tepee! Laugh–I thought Joe was going to pass out, he was laughing so hard!

That night, Joe and I were having dinner with two guys from Brooklyn. Joe decides he is going to tell the joke–oh, no–I thought. Joe begins, laughing as he is telling the joke– Did you hear about the Indian who drank so much tea–he went home and drowned in his own Wigwam! Now, I am howling, along with Joe and the two guys from Brooklyn are looking at each other–I knew what they were thinking–they could understand Joe–but what's wrong with me?

Why don't you go take your shower, Alfie! You had to be there! I was having more fun anyway–Just Thinking.

THE WINNER IS
MOMMIE, MICHAEL

Alfie was staying over at Aunt Rodie's house. It looked like a quiet evening. T.V. was lousy again. Enter–son Michael, the disc–jockey. Since Alfie was not here to play any games with me–I thought–why not–I made his older brother and Mommie play the dictionary game.

I knew it was a bad idea when it took me twenty minutes to explain a game Alfie grasped in two. But, Mommie was going to play and we had to get all the rules straight. I was determined there would be no cheating and I was going to turn the pages to the random word in the dictionary.

We're all set–the order–Michael goes first, then Mommie and me–rotating, à la dart rules, after each word. Remember–the first thing that comes into your mind as it relates to Life, I said.

The words and the answers:

1. *European*–of Europe, its people, a native or inhabitant of Europe.

Answers–Michael, of course–I heard European when you were in the bathroom. It does relate to Life, Dear–just give your answer–Poor people, came the reply–o.k., I said, we have to accept that but I don't understand it–however, I don't think they will find out about it in Europe so it couldn't affect the relationship between our continents. I spoke too quickly on this one and said another Country–and before I could give my great answer relating it to Life, I was shouted down and had to concede–let's go to the next word.

2. *Rudder*–a broad, flat, movable piece hinged to the rear of a ship or aircraft, used for steering. Michael yelled–cruising. Me–has to do with steering or guiding ships from shore to shore to improve human relationships and–"I'd rudder be doing some thing else." Mommie loudly interjected. Not bad dear–but you're forgetting the object of the game.

Next word.

3. *Acrimony*–before we got started on this word, Mommie wanted me to turn to another page, Michael was yelling, cruising, and since I didn't have an answer either, I agreed to cheat–I was loosing control of the game anyway–Next.

4. *Captain*–Kangaroo, shouted Michael–Cruising– said mother and I began my answer–one of the most powerful men wearing a hat and steering a ship, greeting passengers, walking around the ship and conducting ceremonies at the–I had to stop–they were both going to quit!

5. *Coalesce*–cruising, I immediately yelled–might as well join them. Come–on, yelled Mommie–let me turn the page–you don't know how to pick a word, she said–I relented, she took the dictionary and–

6. *Denounce*–Oh, said Mommie, I got a good answer for the word below it–dense. I don't know whether to use denounce or deverbs, said Michael. With that, Mommie quit and Michael left to get ready for work, leaving me sitting by myself, with the brilliant intellectual game I had invented to learn

the meaning of words and make one think of
some Philosophy relating to Life.

Wait a minute–I yelled–we have to have a winner–I
denounce the winner for being *dense*–The Winner is
Mommie, Michael!

IT'S AUNT RODIE, ALFIE

Alfie was crying. What happened, Alfie, I said. Aunt Rodie told him he was a bad boy and she never wanted him to come and visit her again What did you do, Alfie "I broke her favorite vase" Did you do it on purpose "No, I didn't mean to, but I was playing basketball in the house and I knew Aunt Rodie had told me not to—but it was raining outside and I had nothing to do."

Listen, Alfie, aunt Rodie didn't mean what she said. When big people get angry they say things without thinking, and they are sorry afterward.

And you are not a bad boy. You did what you did because you were bored—and weak.

This happens to everybody so don't be hard on yourself. You have to forgive yourself and Aunt Rodie. Even though what was done, was wrong, I know you didn't mean it. And even if you did it on purpose, the important thing is—you are sorry.

Let me try and explain what Father Mulhall taught us in high school. There are three things you must consider when something wrong is done:
1. Was the act itself wrong?
2. Did you think about it?
3. Did you do it anyway—giving *full* consent of your will?

Remember this, since you might make mistakes again—but even if you do something on purpose, you must forgive yourself—it is in the past—have a *firm* purpose of not doing it again. Go easy on yourself and try to understand, the other person has the same problems as you—so go easy on them too—forgive them.

Just a minute, Alfie—I have to answer the phone.

The phone call is for you—It's Aunt Rodie, Alfie.

PEACE OF MIND, ALFIE

Shakespeare said, Alfie "What fools we mortals be." How true. But not really everybody—at least not all the time.

But *some* are their own worst enemies. Someone hurts their feelings. And whatever it was—their mind begins reliving the negative event—over and over and over—

I won't talk to them. I can't believe they did this to me. Wait until I tell everybody what they did. I can't wait to see them again, they will be so hurt when I walk by them etc. etc. etc.

How many hours have been hung up on these bitter feelings. Fools we mortals.

And how about the *overly* self–conscious person. Their mind goes over and over and over—with thoughts of—

How do I look? What will they think of me? I can't think of anything to say. I feel so uncomfortable here. What did you say? I wasn't listening. I know they're talking about me. I wish I were dead, etc. etc. etc.

How many wasted hours have been spent being *overly* self–conscious. Fools we mortals.

And how about *trying* to have no Conscience?—

I'll do it if I want to. Don't tell me what to do. Everybody else does it. There's nothing wrong with it. Charity begins at home (and stays there.). I can't wait to get out of here and get good and drunk (what a goal). Wait until I see him, I'll get him. I am going to be the next executive in this Company and I don't care who gets hurt. I don't have time for that kids—I have to make money. I can't go to Church, I have to sleep all day so I can go out and have a good—time—tonight.

How many wasted hours have been spent on these feelings? Fools we mortals.

And another thing—how about the jilted lover. The *constant* thoughts of the relationship and the rejection.

And if there are children? The *negative thinker* never gives them a thought, unless it is to use them against the other person—to do things for them, so they will 'like me better'. (Children don't understand this nonsense—they love you both!) Fools we mortals.

And some Parents miss out on so many fun times they could have with their children because while they are with them—other thoughts are going—over and over in their mind. Despite this, the children may have fun or—why not spoil the fun—yell at them for nothing—it's their fault you're not having fun too!

How much more fun could have been had *together* if the thoughts were diverted toward the feelings of the children! Sad.

We could go on and on with the negative workings of the mind that is out of control—but why am I bothering to tell you all this, Alfie?

To give you a warning! All of the things I said and anything *negative* that is mulled over in the mind is guaranteed to take away peace. You will *Inherit the Wind*—and a strong wind will rip you apart! Your mind will be so occupied with nonsense and guilt that you won't enjoy many moments in the day—your life will be spent trying to escape from yourself—anyway you can—drugs or whatever—but you can't—sooner or later you will have to *really* look in a mirror.

Will you see a happy person? Will you see in a person who has peace?

And the unkind word or action of such a person–I am talking about *really mean*–is a symptom of someone without peace. Their mind is so occupied with this nonsense and selfishness that it becomes cornered and strikes out, maybe not at anybody in sight–but at the person they feel is inferior!

Ignore Them! For in trying to get even–you will become a clone of them and lose your own peace!

We are all self–conscious, Alfie. There is nothing wrong with that. Actually, there is a lot of fun when somebody gets embarrassed.

And we all feel sad and depressed at times–but don't allow negative thoughts to control you for long periods of time, even an hour may be too long, but never a day, a month or years. I have been talking about the extreme.

However, even if the negative thoughts are not yet extreme, if the *qualities* of a *child* are being lost to any degree the thoughts and actions, which go together, must be controlled–so that–over a period of time, a monster is not created, but instead–slowly but persistently–the mind and being, of a person becoming *like* a child, again.

Becoming *like* a child. And what does that mean?

Anyone who thinks of a child as one who will take his marbles home if he doesn't get his way; one who cries and doesn't know any better–after all–'he is only a child'–if you see only the negative little annoyances, a nuisance–then you haven't been watching and listening. Someday, I'll tell you what a child really is, Alfie. And thank goodness some people have been *like* a child all of their lives!

But how do you become *like* a child? How do you get Peace of Mind?–Pray! And if you don't think this is working–the next thing to do is–Pray! Persistence is what is needed.

I am using a lot of *words* in this conversation, Alfie–but words of advice from any source and the good intention of following them–are not enough to attain peace. You could forget about everything I said and just–Pray.

If I looked at you every day and said we are going to have a conversation, and all I said was, "Pray in your own words and also formal prayers"–and you really did–then you wouldn't need any advice. Peace of mind would come to you. But it doesn't always work like that–the player needs incentive to motivate the attainment of his potential.

However, many who can't read and couldn't understand advice, have peace and are *like* children. It comes naturally to them and a lot of them are probably poor–for–it is the distractions that money can buy–along with *total emphasis on feelings* and the *body*–that–slowly–*take away*–Peace.

So–How to get Peace of Mind–Pray!

And–Help others–do something nice for somebody–even if it is only a kind word.

And–follow your conscience. Don't fight with it–don't rationalize wrong into right–be honest with yourself.

And–Enjoy the many wonderful things to do in the world. Even drink is good if it is done in *Moderation* (good word). Another good old word is *Spontaneous*, more fun is had when it is least expected!

And–get involved with daily *happenings*. Never be *overly* self–conscious. If you have something to say, say it. But don't always be thinking of things to say, just to say something. Listen!–You can have fun listening. Then you might have an opinion and can say what you feel.

There is one more word I must mention, Alfie, before I stop talking. *Attitude!* This is the most important word in what we are talking about.

For, it is not the weak (and we are all that)–the weak who make mistakes–that have to worry–provided we are really sorry and trying–it is those with the *total selfish negative attitude*–that should be concerned, but they're not, because they don't care! Nothing may ever change *some* of them and they could care less what I am saying to you–their thoughts over time have been reversed–when the word nonsense is used–they turn it right back and say this whole conversation is nonsense–because they don't give a damn about anything! They–Alfie–are the real fools! *Sumday comes to all!*

Finally, as I told you once before–the only important thing is *the immediate event before you*–enjoy it–only *doing wrong*, having *thoughts of anxiety*, and *useless pondering* can *destroy*–the moment–the day–the Life!

And allow me one more finally, Alfie. You won't believe this, but I want you to *promise* you will read the *Book of Sirach* or *Ecclesiasticus*, as it is known, found in the Bible. This writing *really says something* and gives the *best advice for all us mortals–and fools we will not be*–for following the advice contained in this great work–along with *prayer*–will help keep–or–bring back–Peace of Mind, Alfie!

YOU WILL BE HEARD, ALFIE

If you get away from bowling, tennis, golf, or any sport–you are no longer good at these games–and often you have been away from the games because you just didn't have that special feeling. The same can happen in the game of life and in particular, with prayer.

The Father, Christ, the Holy Spirit and Mary are persons and if you haven't been talking to any of these persons (and that's what prayer is), you don't know what to say. It is necessary to start off with formal prayer, The Our Father, and slowly build up to being comfortable with your own words in addition to the formal prayer.

None of the above Persons have changed over the years. We have. It takes time to pray like a child again. You can't be in the 10th frame without going through the other nine.

And feeling has nothing to do with it. Do you think the Father doesn't love you because you don't feel anything in prayer? But you're not the only one that ever *felt* rejected. When Christ took on His human nature, that part of Him became so dominant that He cried out "MY God, My God, Why have you forsaken me!"

We need to call on the higher gifts we have, the intellect and will. Don't let the emotion control you–that can become an excuse or a crutch for not doing anything–becoming a self martyr or a totally selfish person.

So start saying your morning and night prayers, again,

Alfie—and pray during the day even though you lost that special feeling. Persistence is what is needed. You will be heard, Alfie.

WHAT'S IT ALL ABOUT?

If I said I wanted to talk to you about yesterday and what you remember about the day, Alfie–you might say–how much fun the whole day was–Turkey, pumpkin pie, games, seeing your grandmother, playing with your nieces and nephew–and you might say something happened that was special to you that I wouldn't even think of. But I remember something–I remember when you told your grandmother–you were no longer a child.

The worst thing to be called, in the mind of a teen–ager, is a child. A child can't wait to do adult things–to become a mature adult–whatever that is. But what is a child, Alfie?

A child–is not worried about tomorrow, is not bothered by yesterday.

Is excited about the world, appreciates everything.

Enjoys a good meal or treat (if you let him).

Can manipulate (but who can refuse).

Loves to sing, loves to be with other kids, loves to play, loves people.

Needs authority–needs guidance. Needs understanding. Needs something to do. Needs love.

Says what's on his mind. Is sincere. Says morning and night prayers.–

And a child is probably a lot more, Alfie, but I just thought of something else I remember and something you wish I would forget.

Remember the day–(you were seven years old)–your older

brother and I were talking as we drove along the highway. He was telling me about a palm reader in Wildwood who told him—he would get married at twenty-three, make a lot of money, etc, etc.—and Michael said—and guess what, Dad, she told me I was a diabetic! "Well, you knew that"—you were quick to reply.—

A child listens, asks questions, accepts answers. Does not doubt.

For a child has something very special—Trust.

So, never be ashamed of being a child, Alfie. Adults wish they were children but they can never go back. But—*that's not true*, Alfie.

Because many years ago, Christ placed a child in the midst of the adults around Him and gave them the instruction to become *like* a child. Christ would not say something that couldn't be done and wasn't the thing to do.

When He told the adults to pray—He said—Our Father—because *we are children in this life and someday in heaven.*

So, don't try to get away from something you are, Alfie—for that's—What's It All About!

Part II

This second part must be dedicated to the following:
My family–

To Kathy–the girl who writes better than I do–How about a series by Anygirl, someday, Kath? "Where's the peanut butter, Terry?!"

To Terry–the perfect homemaker (sorry dear). "Need a razor!"

To Michael–the disc jockey–'Never mind the world, what's Michael been doing lately?' (Shake, son) The man of Steel!

To Matthew Patrickyouknowwhatagin–went to play basketball–"Boogie, boogie, boogie!" Sounds like a great future for you, son.

To Pat–the lady who kept us all together these thirty some odd years (and some not so odd, honey)–Define Lady!

And to my grandchildren, Casey Ann, Age 3, Michael Paul, age 1, and Dana Michelle, age 7 months. We don't even know each other, yet!

Love You all,
Dad and Papa

MUSIC!

Music! What is there about it? It can bring you back to yesterday, forty years ago or more.

Without it—what would driving your car be like? What would a parade be like? How would you dance? What would they sing in kindergarten or an adult home? What would a Broadway show be like?

And how can we remember all the words to a song when we can't even remember the name of the person we just met?

For a song can take us away from the problems of the day and make us feel young again.

What is there about music? I don't know the answer and I can't define the feeling. To express what we feel, I can only think of a song title which sums it up—"Magic Moments"!

And now—something different—I will introduce several new writers who were given the assignment of listing a number of songs and since each song tells a story—it follows that if they weave song titles together—they have a story.

I planned on giving an introduction to each author but only the disc jockey will be introduced—it would take too long trying to be clever with an individual introduction. The writers were clever enough on their own and surprised themselves, in the direction the titles took them.

The real meaning of each story is hidden in the titles, as is that 'special feeling' hidden—in—Music!

AUTHOR'S NOTE – 12/12/89

You will have to believe that this first new author heard of these songs, for he is a disc jockey in real life. He chose the following titles as they came into his mind:

Heaven
Paradise City
Back to Life
Cold Hearted
Never Gonna Give You Up
Causing a Commotion
Every Beat of My Heart
What About Me
I Will Survive
What Kind of Man Would I Be
Man in the Mirror
Power of Love
Silent Night
Joy to the World
How am I Supposed to Live Without You

I Feel For You
Do You Believe in Magic
Into the Night
It Takes Two
Don't Shut Me Out
It's No Crime
High On You
Dangerous
It Would Take a Strong Man
Remember Then
Simply Irresistible
Shining Star
Life in the Fast Lane
Tomorrow People
Joy and Pain

Out of the whole list, I only heard of two, Silent Night and Joy to the world–turn the page–I am proud to introduce him–

THAT'S MY SON
By Him

What About me? With each new day I see the same *man in the mirror* and begin once again *causing commotion* with *every beat of my heart.* Joining a world filled with *tomorrow people, life in the fast lane* becomes inevitable for yet another day in this wonderful place I'd like to call *Paradise City.*

As the day continues on and the sun begins to fade, a *simply irresistible shining star* burns bright, through the *heaven* above. It was then that I first laid my eyes on you. *Do you believe in magic?* I was immediately *high on you* and was taken back by the *power of love.* I wanted to express my happiness and *joy to the world* but then *what kind of man would I be* to express that feeling on a rather calm and *silent night.* Well, let me tell you it *would take a strong man* to let such a *dangerous* emotion such as love, hide until two share in the same *joy and pain.* However, I *remember then*, it takes two to make things right. We then go deeper and deeper, still, *into the night* and reality begins to set in on what may have all along been just a dream. Please *don't shut me out. It's no crime* to feel that part of me is *never gonna give you up.* And finally, as a new sun begins to rise, I ask myself *how am I supposed to live without you?* Well, to answer without being down right *cold hearted, I feel for you*, but me, *I will survive.* The new day is now here and it's time for me to get *back to life.*

HER WAY

by Kathy

Even Now
Teach Your Children
Twist and Shout
Longer Than
Big Girls Don't Cry
I Wanna Hold Your Hand
Forever
Amazing Grace
Precious and Few
Impossible Dream
Cherish
Memories
Bad
Bicycle Built for Two
Under the Boardwalk
Always a Woman
Lady
School Days
The Morning After
Time is Flowing Like a
   River

Louie Louie
My Way
9 to 5
Hello Again
The Eeensy Weensy Spider
Be Not Afraid
Money
American Pie
Knocking on Heaven's Door
O Come All ye Faithful
Heaven Knows
Work Hard for Your
   Money
Material Girl
Wild Thing
Somewhere Over the
   Rainbow
Don't Worry, Be Happy
I Am, I Said
I Write the Songs
Working for a Living

Assignment. Almost 30 years old and my father even now is telling me what to do! Is that so wrong. . . does he have the right? We're told to *teach your children* well. I don't want to *twist and shout* about it. How long do we teach them. . . *Longer than* a lifetime? I sure hope so. Now I know *that big girls don't cry* but what is wrong if *I wanna hold your hand forever.*

And now I'm a parent, *amazing grace,* (don't ask "who's Grace" you know what I mean). Moments with your children are *precious and few.* It is an *impossible dream* to last and soon the moments we *cherish* will only be *memories.* I guess that's not so *bad,* at least if you're an optimist. That *bicycle built for two under the boardwalk* (alright maybe it was on the boardwalk but it's my memory) was a blast! You can forget about the big fight your brother and sister had and how you had to come to the rescue and ride in the back seat. Oh well, I guess I was *always a woman.*

Anyway, I better get to the assignment. Cheat? Me? Not a *lady.* Well, alright, maybe I did put a few songs in that weren't on my original list. And maybe I let my husband give me some ideas for variety. Now what was that assignment again?

As I remember back in my *school days* I would do my homework as soon as I was assigned—even terms of endearment (songs, Kathy, not movies) sorry, I mean term papers—I would get them done within the first couple of weeks even if the due date was at the end of the semester. And here, I sit the night before my father wants this, actually getting to be *the morning after* the night before. And now that I'm *working for a living, time is flowing like a river* (boy I wish my hours were *9 to 5.* I'd have another song, not to mention an extra 30 minutes to get ready!)

So why have I changed so much? Priorities or procrastinations? I think I'll take a break. *Hello again!* only kidding. I guess it's a little of both and after all aren't they partners in crime (there must be a song named that).

Anyway, I guess I would have to say priorities have changed. I talk to my girlfriends about grocery stores and diaper prices and I actually enjoy watching Sesame Street and singing the *eensy weensy spider*. And although my husband says *be not afraid*, I feel compelled to worry about *money*. I guess no matter how you slice the *American pie*, no matter what situation you are in, financial security is *knocking on heavens door*.

I know we're supposed to *O come all ye faithful but heaven knows you have to work hard for your money*. I'd like to think I'm not a *material girl*. It never mattered before. . . but I never had a mortgage, car loans, grocery and doctor bills to pay. A *wild thing* can happen when you stop the worrying and let the cliches such as "life is too short" really sink in. After all He will provide *somewhere over the rainbow. Don't worry, be happy*. You know what? *I am*, I said I really am.

Oh no, speaking of procrastination, I have to get back to the assignment. I just don't know if I'll be able to do it. *I write the songs*, I mean the poems in the family. I can't write a story reflecting life using song titles. How do you use *Louie Louie* (not my tune) to describe the meaning of Life. Oh well, I'll just have to tell dad I'll do it *my way*.

RAISING A FAMILY
By "The Typist"

Midnight Train to Georgia
Money
Make Me Feel So Good
Back to Life
Life Goes On

The Beat Goes on
Wedding Song
Daddy's Little Girl
Yesterday

Celebrate
School's Out For Summer
Just the Way You Are

Just You and I
We are Family
Work Hard for a Living
When I See You Smile
We Live in a Material
    World
Parents Just Don't
    Understand
Impossible Dream
Longer Than
Be not Afraid
If You Don't Know Me By
    Now
I am Woman
Wish I were 18 Again

It used to be just *you and I* but now *we are family*. I *work hard for a living* but it's all worthwhile *when I see you* (and the girls) *smile*. The big problem today is that *we live in a material world* (here I go—is that a title or just part of a song). Our *parents just don't understand* this sometimes. When they think of how they scrimped and saved to just get by and how we have a house, two cars, two T.V.'s, etc.

To them it was just an *impossible dream*. It took them *longer than* it took us. You always tell me *be not afraid*, everything will work out. I guess you're right–it usually does, but *if you don't know me by now*, I sometimes have to worry. It might be because *I am Woman*.

I didn't know where I was going to go from here, but I wrote the first part of this *yesterday* and typed my sister's today. I can't believe we were on the same *Midnight train* (of thought) *to Georgia* (I know I'm pushing it but!). I thought I was the only one who worried about where the *money* was going to come from. It *makes me feel so good* (that might be "brand new"–I've had this problem all my life–remember, Precious and Sue!). I told you I wasn't good with titles. Well, let's get *back to life*.

I can't believe *life goes on* so fast. We'll be singing *Happy Birthday* to Casey for the fourth time and to Dana for the first time in a few months. The *beat goes on!* Before you know it, we'll be singing the *wedding song* and *daddy's little girl* for our kids and then we'll *wish we were 18 again*. It seems like only *yesterday* when we would *celebrate* when *schools out for summer*.

Well, I guess I cheated too because I did fill in as I went along. At least I finished it! It's better than nothing. Just remember Dad, I love you *just the way you are*–even though you're fat!

NO PROBLEM

by Matthew

Workin' for a Living
Don't Worry Be Happy
Faith
Opposites Attract
Back in the Highlife
Back in Time
Blame it on the Rain
Life in the Fast Lane
Forever in your Heart

Just the Way You Are
Big Shot
Miss You Much
Finish What You Started
Vacation
No One is to Blame
In Your Room
Break Down the Walls
That's All

Do you have a problem? Well *don't worry be happy have faith* and maybe you'll be *back in the high life again.* If you think all is hopeless remember *back in time* when you were *in your room* thinking of someone or something that was to be *forever in your heart.* You felt pretty good, I'll bet. Now that you look back, it probably felt like *life in the fast lane.* Things can be just as good if you can just *break down the walls,* that are keeping you inside.

If you're *workin' for a living* take a *vacation* and if you feel bad *blame it on the rain* and forget about it. You don't have to be a *big shot* for someone to *miss you much* because I like you *just the way you are.*

No one is to blame even *opposites attract.* So if you *finish what you started* and do the best you can, then *that's all* anyone can ask for. And if someone wants more, then maybe they're the one with the problem.

"SHOES"

by Roz

After reading your dissertation, my songs are:

Silent Night
Walking My Baby Back
    Home
Love is Driving Me
    Bananas
Life is Just a Bowl of
    Cherries

I'm Gonna Sit Right Down
    and Write Myself a
    Letter
Chattanooga Choo–Choo
My Baby Smiled at Me

It was a *silent night* and I was *walking my baby back home* when I heard the *Chattanooga Choo–Choo*. When *My baby smiled at me*, I realized that *life is just a bowl of cherries* and when I get home *I'm gonna sit right down and write myself a letter* since *love is driving me bananas*.

Another comment by Anyman–Whoever heard of "Love Is Driving Me Bananas"? What a coincidence! It was my great, great grandfathers favorite song!

DENISE

By Guess Who

All of Me
Always
You Always Hurt the One
    You Love
Unforgettable
There Must Be a Way
One in a Million

To Each His own Crazy

I Fall to Pieces
In the Mood
All Dressed up with a
    Broken Heart
Leave Me Alone

As *always*, Saturday night is coming, invited out to dinner and have nothing to wear. Now I need to go shopping and buy new clothes for *all of me*. *There must be a way* for me to find the perfect outfit, so away I go to the mall. I'm always *in the mood* to shop. The dress that I wanted was so expensive that I asked the sales girl if she was *crazy*. She said no, that this dress was *one in a million* and that if I wore it I would have an *unforgettable* evening. I bought the dress and started to look for shoes to match. The clerk at the shoe store did not agree with my choice and said *to each his own* lady and shook his head as I left. When I got home I was anxious to try on my new clothes and the dog would not *leave me alone*, he wanted to play. Every time I scolded him he just sat there and looked at me with those big sad eyes and made me feel so bad, that I gave him a hug and said I was sorry. It seemed like he understood when I said *you always hurt the one you love* and was his playful self again. Finally, I'm dressed and ready to go, and just in time. As we drive away I'm thinking of the sales girl's remark and hope that at nights end, I won't be *all dressed up with a broken heart.*

UNTIL IT'S TIME FOR YOU TO GO
By A Friend of N.D.

Stargazer
Lonely Looking Sky
Beautiful Noise
Done Too Soon
Headed for the Future
Brother Love's Traveling
    Salvation Show
Serenade
I've Been This Way Before
Thank the Lord for the
    Nighttime
This Time

Red Red Wine
Brooklyn Roads
Coldwater Morning
Solitary Man
America
September Morn
Skybird
Summerlove
Love on the Rocks
Hello Again
The Best Years of our Lives

    I'm the *stargazer* in the family. Tonight I'm sitting on our porch thinking and sipping a little *red red wine*. It's a *lonely looking sky* to me. We're moving again. This isn't the first time it's happened. We've traveled *Brooklyn roads* and left the *beautiful noise* of the city as well as the countryside of Connecticut and the *coldwater morning* of Upstate. It's always *done too soon* and we move on.

    Since my husband isn't a *solitary man* and again is *headed for the future* with his company, I'm packing our bags another time. After all this is *America* and he's moving up the corporate ladder. I should remember what it's like;

I've been part of *brother love's traveling salvation show* for 25 years now. It's always hard to leave a place you've gotten used to and leave the friends you've made to start over.

There was many a *September morn* spent at the lake, the *sky—bird* flitting down to the water and the sweet *serenade* of children laying that are etched in my memory, leaving a feeling of a sweet *summerlove* for years spent here. *I've been this way before* so I'll deal with it. Look, if I hadn't moved here I would have this feeling of *love on the rocks* now.

In the meantime I'll *thank the Lord for the nighttime*. It gives me a chance to sort my feelings. Tomorrow I'll be ready to move on and say *hello again*. After all these are *the best years of our lives*, and I intend to make the most of it. *This time* will be even better.

A RING OF TRUTH

by Rick

So I'm sitting home *all by myself* one evening when the phone rings and it happens to be a call from my friend, Anyman. He wants me to play a game, so *help me Rhonda* this is true, a song game at that where I list songs and then make up a story. Well, *this is it*.

Happy Together
Dancing in the Street
My Generation
This is It
Bus Stop
My Girl
Cloudy
Sunday Morning
Satisfaction
Is it any Wonder
On a Carousel
I'm a Better man
All You Need is Love
Footloose
Born to Run
Making Every Minute
Count

All By Myself
Let Me Be
Sooner or Later
Borderline
Faith
Joy to the World
Fool on the Hill
Scarborough Fair
Midnight Hour
Gotta Get Away
God Only Knows
Just One Look
Respect
For What It's Worth
Help Me Rhonda

Keep the Fire Burning

It was early *Sunday morning* on a *cloudy* day, when me and *my girl* were waiting at the *bus stop* for the crosstown bus to take us to the annual *Scarborough fair*. The girl and I are so *happy together* that anyone could take *just one look* at us and see that in this world *all you need is love* to make things happen or make you feel like *dancing in the street*. The others here appeared so somber and austere but just our existence should make you feel so full of *joy to the world* that even if you feel like you *gotta get away* you have to *keep the fire burning* within yourself any way possible.

I can say this, for I once acted like a *fool on the hill* because in being part of *my generation* of the late 60's, I felt I was free to do whatever I wanted including staying way out well past the *midnight hour* and not even my parents could stop me for I was *born to run*. I showed little *respect* for authority figures and wished everybody would *let me be* to do my own thing *for what it's worth*.

Is it any wonder that once you become older and hopefully wiser that one gleans a certain satisfaction, to withstand all the pressure of being a child of the Hip Generation" who was advised to tune in, turn on and drop out". I thought—I could maintain my *foot—loose*, carefree lifestyle but *sooner or later* I came to realize this is a *borderline* existence at best and *faith* straightened me out. *God only knows* there is a lot to *making every minute count* but I don't feel I'm *on a carousel* anymore and hopefully *I'm a better man* than I was as a youth.

As I read this over again, maybe my story has a ring of truth to it Alfie.

Part III
(For Catholics)

ONCE, IN TIME, ALFIE

Once upon a time, Alfie, there were two kings. One was King of Myland and the other was King of Timeland. The King of Timeland had been given his kingdom by King Myland and his kingdom was vast. There were many subjects and many problems. This King was afraid to offend King Myland but also afraid to offend any of his subjects. He became a liberal King–No discipline–No laws–his subjects could do whatever they wanted.

One day, the Timeland people invaded the other kingdom. They destroyed and stole much of the property–King Myland was angered.

The Timeland people were summoned to the Palace for a meeting with their King for he knew his kingdom may be destroyed. The King was afraid to face King Myland–so he ordered gifts and messages sent from the wisest men in his kingdom but he could not appease The King.

Finally, he decided he would go himself to make up for the wrongs of his subjects. King Myland was satisfied. It took some one on the same level–King to King–to assure peace in the kingdoms.

We are people who live in Time, Alfie. If our Country offended Russia, would we send a dog with a note of apology around his neck to make–up? Would we send one of our famous prisoners? Or should we send our President–someone who is a person of the country that made the offense and on an equal par with the head of the Country offended?

Years ago, Alfie, still in Time, the Creator of man was offended by man. This was a problem for man but the Creator had the answer. Man, not being on a par with the Creator could never make–up for the offense. So the Creator, whom we call God, sent His son to become man.

Thus, God who was offended was appeased by man, the offender, and by someone of an equal par with Him–a God–MAN.

We even date our Calendar from the birth of this God–Man–Jesus Christ–who was born almost 2000 years ago, now–Once, In Time, Alfie.

WE ARE ALL ONE

The priest was preparing for his first sermon. The Pastor would be in the Congregation, his parents, his friends and with his luck, a lot of new parishioners who didn't want to be there. It was the first Sunday Mass of the combined Churches due to the shortage of priests. It didn't matter. He had prepared this sermon a long time ago.

As he reviewed what he had written, he was impressed again with his historical masterpiece, weaving statements together with brilliant logic, linking the Old Testament with the New and concluding with a reference to the Mystical Body.

The phone rang. The voice of an old lady asked for the time of the Mass. She stated how she had hoped this day would never come. The Parish in which she and her daughter had been married no longer existed. Her daughter was not coming. neither was her granddaughter who was to be married in 'their Church'. She received the approval to live together with her fiancé. What difference did it make now? To be married in the same Church as her mother and grandmother could never be.

"Why are you coming?" Father asked. There was a second of silence and the old lady replied, "My prayer didn't change the reality of the time but Christ will be there and that's where I want to be."

Father hung up the phone. He was no longer impressed

with his prepared sermon. His mind was blank as he walked to the Altar and soon to the Pulpit.

"In the Name of the Father, and of the Son and of the Holy Spirit," he began. "I am going to be brief. There is a lady present who didn't come to hear me. She told me she was coming because Christ will be here at the Consecration.

I want to say something to her. Keep praying. Sometimes we pray so hard and long for something, that we question our Faith when we don't get what we want. Keep praying.

Only, pray for your family. Pray for some poor sinner in close proximity to you. Pray for the person who is dying not far from you, that they may make it, at least, into Purgatory. Pray for peace. Pray for the end to abortions.

Pray in your own words and pray the Rosary every day for people in need. For the reality of the time is the same in the church today, as it was when Christ started the Church. Prayer was needed then as it is now, for others as well as for ourselves. For the goal of heaven is the same for all and the power of prayer should never be underestimated!

But we in this Church, today, are not Italian, Polish and Irish who came because the Jewish man, Christ is here. *We are people* who came because the *God–Man*, Christ, is here.

I will now continue the Mass and not make this lady wait any longer. Let's pray with her.

We are all one!"

DIVINE ROCK, ALFIE

Alfie and I were on vacation. It was the first time he had flown. He was excited. I was trying to be cool, as I heard a child say. Rome wasn't built in a day–someone on the plane remarked–talk about trying to be cool!

Finally, we landed and spent five days in Rome, hearing and reliving moments from the past–seeing the still beautiful sights of the present and just as Rome wasn't built in a day–before you could blink an eye–I was trying to be cool again–up in the clouds.

What did you think of the Pope, Alfie, I said? I wanted to ask him why he won't change things like Aunt Rodie says he should, Alfie replied. Aunt Rodie, I thought–so that's it–she is always talking about abortion and other things–someday we will get a Pope who will change everything–you'll see–was what his aunt was hoping–a Pope who would think like she does.

No, Alfie, I said, the Pope didn't make the laws Aunt Rodie is talking about–he never said–Thou shalt not kill or Thou shalt not commit adultery–he never said many other things that Aunt Rodie wants changed–these are Divine Laws, law of God.

You see, Christ made Peter the first Pope because He wanted a leader who would be firm and have the last say in what God wants and knows we need. If He left doctrine up to us–we would have a lot more churches than we do today.

No, Alfie, He did not say–upon you I will build *your Church*–He said–Thou art rock and upon this rock I will build *my church!*

The Pope cannot change the law of God because it would be easier for some people to accept. The Pope must be firm in the doctrine of Christ–Divine Rock, Alfie!

WHAT CHANGES, ALFIE?

Alfie was not himself. Walking home from Church he was silent. Let's stop in the diner, I said. Nothing like pancakes and sausage to raise your spirits or something else!

Ok, Alfie, what's the problem? It was Aunt Rodie again. Is it true, Alfie asked, that the Church changes all the time. He had heard Aunt Rodie talking with her Bingo friends on how the Church wasn't like it used to be and wait until you see all the new changes–Did you hear, etc, etc. . .

What changes, Alfie, I said? The Church still teaches that there are three persons in God–that one person is called the Father–that the person of Christ is in the Blessed Sacrament–that Christ was conceived by the person known as the Holy Spirit–that Mary is still the virgin mother of Christ (the God–Man)–that Christ suffered and died for our sins so we can go to heaven some day–and many other things. There are still 10 commandments, the forgiveness of sins, the same Holy Days of Obligation and the Church still teaches love, prayer and the mass are the most important things we can do. And guess what Alfie, they still shovel the sidewalk in front of the Church.

No, Alfie, the Church could never change. The way of doing things might change but *no basic truth* can ever be changed.

Could I have some more sausage, Alfie asked? Why not I said–that could be the link you need!

RECEIVING THE HOST, ALFIE

We were on the way home from Church and Alfie was silent. What's the matter, Alfie, I said? He felt bad because he was *bored* in church and felt he should have paid more attention at Mass. You're right, Alfie–you should pay attention but you didn't do anything wrong–it is hard to pay attention. You must *think* of what is happening.

Years ago, the nuns taught us that there were four reasons why we attend Mass and these reasons do not change:

1. To adore God as Our Father.
2. To thank Him for all things.
3. To say you're sorry for any wrong you did and sorry for the wrong done by other people.
4. To ask for things for yourself *and others.*

It is necessary to get to Church a little early and prepare for what is about to happen by *thinking and praying* about these four reasons. But how, Alfie?

Years ago also, Alfie, Don McNeil, on the old 'Breakfast Club', a radio show would pause, music would play, while he waited for a minute in silence, after giving the request to his audience–"Each in his own word, each in his own way, bow your heads and let us pray."

That is the way to prepare for mass and what is about to happen–for at Mass, something special happens. It is a mystery–something we believe but can't fully understand. At the Consecration, Christ comes through the power of

God and the words of the Priest, into the Host, under the appearance of bread.

God wants *all people* to go to heaven and also to be happy here. He gives sufficient help to *all people*, in some way, to accomplish this.

However, just as a good parent *wants to be with his children*, Christ wanted to be with *people* in a special way.

Almost two thousand years ago, he walked on earth and was seen. To remain on earth and walk around for two thousand years and more would not make much sense and would not make him a normal man who lives for a time. Seeing would not be believing.

There might be a number of ways he could be with people—and *in some way* he helps *all people*—but he told his Apostles he would be present in bread, the Host, and gave them the instruction to say the words for this to happen.

So, the next time we go to Mass, Alfie, remember the four reasons given by the nuns—prepare—and remember also, you do not go to Communion because *you are good*—you go to Communion, *to be good*—for just as people received help from Christ, almost two thousand years ago—and just as *all people* receive help *in some way*, to be good today—for us, as Catholics, that way is by—Receiving the Host, Alfie.

BACK TO THE RECTORY, ALFIE

When we were walking home from Church yesterday, we were talking about the Mass, Alfie and the presence of Christ in the Host. I wanted to say more but felt I talked long enough.

I believe, that Christ is in the Blessed Sacrament. Remember when I told you about the Clock and Creation, Alfie. That is so simple to see with logic and just common–sense, but the presence of Christ in the Host is one of our mysteries. We don't need to explain it. It is a matter of Faith.

Besides, how God could ever do such a thing, is too difficult a question. For how could the Creator, The Father, Son and Holy Spirit (Trinity, another mystery)–the makers of the sun, the stars, a tree, a flower, the animals, the planets, and man himself–and all these things with their intricate parts and control and order–I ask again, how could these Persons have the power, to send the Son, Christ, to be present in the Host under the appearance of bread, if they wanted to?

It is a lot easier to create a Universe than to appear in a Host–isn't it, Alfie? *But I believe.*

It is so much easier to answer things here on earth. We know how things happen.

Like–how a person can be seen on every T.V. in the Country, at the same time, by coming thru wires and even thru the air, via satellite, all over the world, and appearing live, under the appearance of a picture! The answer—the power of electricity.

The appearance of the person in the form of a picture is due to the property of *certain* fundamental particles of all matter, as electrons (negative charges) and protons or positrons (positive charges) and this *electrical* charge is generated by friction, induction or chemical change. And you do not see the electricity! This, *I also believe!*

But—how could the—Never mind—

But getting back to the Host, Alfie. Let me tell you a *true* story. This really happened!

I was collecting for the Bishop's Fund, driving from block to block to the houses on my list. At the one house, an elderly lady said she didn't have time—I told her, O.K., and started away—she called me back. Now this woman who was contributing five dollars of her money to the Fund had time—I mean—she had time! I heard the history of the family—she even brought out the pictures and insisted I eat some old candy (which I didn't want)—and this candy must have been on the table since the last person collected.

Finally, I was just about out the door—when she said—"Could I ask you something?" Sure, go ahead.

She asked what you would do if the Host dropped on the floor at Communion time? I gave her a standard answer—then she told me she was assigned to give out Communion at Mass, dropped a Host on the floor by accident, put it in her hankie and brought it home—and before I could say anything—she went into the kitchen and brought in the Host, asking me to take it back!

I said—o.k.—but could she put it in something for me to carry it in. Back to the kitchen she went and back again with a baggie, stamped with a picture of Mickey Mouse, and the Host inside! Oh, and she also had an apple for me.

At this point, I am stunned—and realize—I am standing

in the doorway with an apple and a five dollar check in one hand, and the Host, in a Mickey Mouse bag, in the other! I thanked her and left.

Never refer to a person as it, Alfie. Sometimes we do, when talking about a mystery—but I think the person understands.

I didn't go on any more calls that day, Alfie. I got into my car and started to drive. There was total silence in the car—both persons were quiet. But, somehow, I knew, this was the greatest honor of my life—the day I drove Him—Back To The Rectory, Alfie.

BRAND M, ALFIE?

My mind was wondering. I couldn't wait to get home and I knew Alfie felt the same way. Why is the priest talking so long? Why did we oversleep? We could be late. If only we had made the early Mass. What is he saying? Something about Mary?. . .

Finally, we are walking home at a fast pace. But wait, I was wrong. Alfie was listening to the priest for he asked– "How important is Mary?" I slowed my pace. What if we were late for the rodeo show. What can I tell him?

Well, Alfie, I said, if you think of the Brand X rodeo, (which was all I could think about), you may understand. You see, the owner brands all his animals with an X because they belong to him and are very special.

The Creator has made Mary very special. She is the mother of Christ. She is the person in heaven who intercedes for all mankind!

Look at the palm of your hands. What do you see? Did the Creator brand us as His through Christ and Mary? Look again! Brand M, Alfie?

THE PERFECT TIME
TO BEGIN, ALFIE

Authors Note: Again, I ask for those who are not Roman Catholic to bear with me. At this writing, many Catholics are going to Medjugorje. National TV (20/20) recently had a special regarding reports of apparitions.

Somebody asked me what I thought of Medjugorje, Alfie? And you know what–I can't answer that question.

The Church will eventually give the answer. But did you ever hear of Fatima?

Fatima–this we do know. What's that, you ask, Alfie?

Mary appeared to three children, in 1917, in Portugal, and gave them a message. But that was 72 years ago! So– does that mean we shouldn't follow the message of Christ because it was given over 1900 years ago?

The following are some of the key things that were said to Lucia, (a child in Fatima who later became a nun) during the period between 1917 and 1942:

1) "I promise to assist at the hour of death with the graces necessary for salvation all those who, on the first Saturday of five consecutive months, go to confession and receive Holy Communion, recite the Rosary and keep me company for a quarter of an hour while meditating on the mysteries of the Rosary with the intention of making reparation to me."

2) "Say the Rosary, inserting between the mysteries the following ejaculation–'O my Jesus, forgive us. Save us from the fire of Hell. Bring all souls to Heaven, especially those in most need.' "

3) "I am the Lady of the Rosary–say the Rosary ever day"

4) "Pray! Pray a great deal and make sacrifices for sinners–"

5) And later, Christ told Lucia what He wanted–'The sacrifices required of every person is the fulfillment of his duties in life and the observance of My law. This is the penance that I now seek and require!'

6) And earlier, the prayer of the angel, "My God, I believe, I adore, I hope, and I love You. I beg pardon of You for those who do not believe, do not adore, do not hope, and do not love You."

Yes, we do know Fatima, Alfie. Read any books on Fatima and notice the Nihil Obstat and Imprimatur of the church. The above statements are found in–"The Crusade of Fatima", by John De Marchi, published by P. J. Kenedy & Sons, New York.

Read about the 'Miracle of the Sun' in several Secular papers in Portugal–reported by assigned journalists who were at Fatima, including the "O Dia" and O Seculo" of Lisbon–in which the newspaper men and an estimated 70,000 to 100,000 people witnessed this event. Part of the statement in "O Seculo" (which goes into detail) said–"the sun trembled and made some brusque unheard of movements beyond all cosmic laws." The sun was said to have "danced" and came toward the crowd changing colors. It could be seen without the normal difficulty when one tried to stare directly at it and shortly before, it had been raining but at the end of this event–the clothes of the people were dry.

There were too many who witnessed this to cause any doubt as to the happening!

And one more thing, Alfie. In 1917, it was reported by the child Lucia what else Mary said. She asked for "the consecration of Russia to my Immaculate Heart." And said further, "Russia will be converted, and there will be peace," if her requests were heeded!

Read the book–converted to what–Democracy, Christianity, Catholicism? We will see some day.

I remember in grammar school, the nuns asking us to follow the requests of Fatima. You pray for what you are told–even the impossible. But never did it look possible for what we are seeing today!

Now is *not* the time to stop praying for peace, Alfie. Say the rosary everyday and make the First Saturdays (as Our Lady of Fatima requested). For–this year and every year for 72 times 72–is–The Perfect Time To Begin, Alfie!

Part IV

WHY NOT TRY, ALFIE?

I can't believe it, Alfie! I have been telling our conversations to some people and they want to hear more. But on what subject? It reminds me of that program we used to watch, "It pays to be Ignorant."

The statement from the moderator is–the Bible contains the best written facts of all time–Question to the panel of two–what book contains the best written facts?

The experts–in conversation. My mother read a book once–Oh, yea, where?–In Pittsburgh–Pittsburgh!–I used to work in that town–Really, I tried to work once in a diner–How much did you make?–Oh, about thirty or forty orders a day–Speaking of forty, my birthday is next week–Oh, will you be forty?–No–but I thought maybe I could get a free order from the diner.

Finally,–Moderator–will you guys come on–answer the question!

Well, Alfie, I guess the answer is that I can't think of any more to talk about. But if you read this far–turn the page. Why not try, Alfie.

HODGE PODGE, ALFIE

I brought some pages home from some old desk calendars, Alfie. When I hear something I like, I write it down.

Some of the things are good and some are—well you decide, Alfie.

Aristotle—"The mind as created is as sensitive to the truth, as the eye to the light, or the ear to sound."

From the movie—He that troubleth his own heart—Inherits the Wind!

From the office—

Pondering—fishing by a Pond.

Cheap—avoid all sales and save the money.

Cold (and cheap)—find an artist to draw a fire place and sit near it.

Oh well, they never were very funny at the office.

Mother Teresa—"We can do no great things; only small things with great love."

Perfection—what Mother Teresa said.

Problem—the girl down the street, husband left her, two small children, works to support them, diabetic, and just diagnosed with a condition that requires a diet different from the diabetic diet.

Problem,— —

(Fill in some problem you know.)

Problem,–(space for your problem)

Unknown Author–Rise above the temptation to fear, to discouragement and to sadness, this distrust paralyzes* your activities. Be Serene! Be Calm! And Joyous!

Fear–useless, what is needed is Trust.

Comment–Nobody likes a whiner or a wino.

Comment–"I never made a mistake–I thought I did once–but I was wrong." (Monday night football–Howard Cosell).

Father Peyton–"More things are wrought by prayer than this world dreams of."

Father Peyton–"The family that prays together, stays together."

Principle–the end does not justify the means (example)– The *good purpose* of protecting the feelings of the mother does not justify using the means of *killing* the baby inside of her.

St. Teresa (Little Flower)–I busy myself, not with things great, nor with things sublime!

Emerson–The reward of a thing well done–is to have done it.

Epitaph–"I told you I was sick!"

Math–Count the years by the smiles not the tears.

Advice to children–Never talk to strangers, unless they are wearing Red Sox hats–then you know they are Good Guys.

Camelot (King to the boy ready to fight) We are all like drops of water which make the ocean–but some of the drops sparkle!

Thomas Merton–In essence–To do your will, Father, I may be confused and not always sure–but I am sure I desire to please you–and sure this is pleasing to You–and thus, somehow, I will be led on the right path.

And finally, the comment of Peter Jennings to end the

tragic news of 6/5/89–China, Iran, Congress and then–a class reunion of a bunch of adults, after thirty years, making fools of themselves on National T.V.

Said Jennings,

"Thank God for the sane people in the world!"

AMEN–to that!

Hodge Podge, Alfie.

THE DAY OFF, ALFIE

Do you have to work today, Dad? Of course I do, Alfie. Why do you ask?

Alfie had the day off from school and I knew he wanted to spend the day doing something with me. Well, maybe not the whole day but at least part of the day–the part of the day and time it would take to drive him and his friends to the Mall to see "The Future Is Backward," or something like that.

Do you realize the chaos it could cause if we all took the day off anytime we pleased? Let me tell you a story, Alfie.

There once was a County called, Watchit, and this County was different from the other Counties in the State. Every City and every little town and village had their own traffic rules and were allowed to pick any colors they wanted, to control traffic. It was the idea of Mayor Buddie Pleaseemall. His city had different color traffic lights–Stop and Go–every other block!–Stop on purple, go on blue, on one street–stop on green, go on red on another and visa versa on the next corner. He even allowed the top light to be the go light and the bottom light to mean stop–every other block.

When people from other countries drove through Watchit County, there were many accidents because they didn't abide by the traffic rules! It was no problem for the people that lived in the area–they all learned to walk, since most of the cars in the Community had been totaled!

Finally, the Governor of the State had to tell the Mayor that his County had to comply with the rest of the State. This happened after the Governor himself drove through the County with his Chauffeur and suffered severe neck problems, from quick stops. It was that day the Governor learned his chauffeur was color blind!

So, he sent a message to the mayor that he would be impeached if he didn't comply—in the exact words of the Governor—watchit Buddie!

I must be honest with you, Alfie, what I told you didn't really happen. But seriously, think about it—can you imagine what our City would be like if everybody did whatever they wanted and we didn't have any laws?

Can you imagine what the World would be like if there were no Commandments or no conscience given by the Creator to give man the sense of right and wrong? We have enough problems even with these facts but what if nobody cared what they did or who they hurt?

At least most of the people in the world are good!

Well, with all this talk, I am going to be late for work. Why don't you call your friends? Maybe, I will take—The Day Off, Alfie.

CASEY ANN, 12/6/89

This is not made up folks:

Casey Ann, my granddaughter, age 3, was staying overnight. Our dog Crystal was sleeping. Said Casey Ann, to her uncle, "Maybe I can get a Crystal for my birthday". Her uncle said, Oh, you want a dog of your own. "Yes, after my bird dies." You have a bird? "Not yet", came the reply.

I should stop there with that one–but I got to get into the act. Earlier, my wife had just made me a cup of coffee and noticing the time–I rushed out to the little store around the corner. My wife put the coffee cup in the microwave for me.

Later, Casey Ann got a 'boo–boo' (whoever thought of that word) and was crying. Enter, Pa–Pa. Wait until you see my magic trick–I said. And after all the antics of the master magician–I opened the microwave and Wa–La!

Casey was amazed and wanted me to do it again. Maybe next time when you come over, I replied. I don't want anymore coffee now.

That night, Casey Ann came 'special' to me and said– Good–night Pa–Pa.

Maybe, we are finally getting to know each other–well at least, I am getting to know her–for the coffee will be in the microwave the next time I see–Casey Ann.

CHANGE THE SUBJECT OR THE OBJECT, ALFIE

Turn off the T.V., Alfie. Wait until you hear this! A couple of days ago, right down the block, Alfie, something fell out of the sky. There it was, in the middle of Mr. Pittfall's yard. It was round and seemed to change colors. All the people in the neighborhood gathered together, even the couple across the street who never speak to anyone.

It is an orange meteorite, someone said–another agreed but thought it was red–yet another said it looked more like a garnet star. The discussion continued and there were so many opinions, everyone was confused. Mr. and Mrs. Cautious became frightened and ran home. Mr. Pittfall invited everybody into his house, and they phoned the police.

James and Gary, Mr. Pittfall's children, were watching all the activity from high above, hiding behind the limb of an old maple tree they were forbidden to climb.

The police came and after throwing a blanket over the object, one of them carried it away. They still haven't said what it is–but I bet James and Gary had something to do with it.

The whole thing reminds me of school, Alfie, and something else nobody seems to understand. We learned about Objective and Subjective facts. The Objective fact is something that exists outside the mind. It can be material of immaterial. The Subjective fact is what the Subject or person perceives the object to be, what it is or what it isn't. However, what the person thinks does not always correspond with the reality of what the object is. But regardless of what any person thinks, the fact of the object being there remains and the object either is or isn't something. I'll bet you can't wait to get this in school, Alfie.

The point is, if there is an apple on the sidewalk, it doesn't matter if somebody says it's an orange in the middle of the road. The fact is—it's an apple on the sidewalk.

Likewise, there is a truth, an answer to everything and what ever the truth is, it cannot be changed, it is the objective fact. The subject or person can use logic and perceive the truth to be whatever they want it to be—but that will never change the fact of what the truth really is.

The basic make—up of people is the same today as it was thousands of years ago and the truths and moral values can never change anymore than the basic need for food and water. These are objective facts of the human race. It is people who try to change the objective facts to fit their own Subjective demands.

You know what is right and wrong, Alfie. The ten commandments are objective facts—never try to be a clever thinking Subject to change these or any other facts you have learned. Also, never judge anybody who does wrong—you never know what is in the mind of the Subject. The action done can never change as being wrong, but the Subject may not be guilty of any wrong in his own mind (if sincere, with no rationalization). But the Subject can change and recognize the truth.

And don't get confused if you see a *known truth* or *doctrine* challenged by a brilliant intellectual. Just remember that some facts are not always completely understood but it is difficult for the Intellectual to admit there is something they don't understand.

Also, don't be upset if an elected official or a church leader are not living the way they should. The Constitution and the Bible cannot be questioned because the subjects who are appointed to uphold them act in ways inconsistent with the content of these great works.

Never try to change the objective fact, Alfie. Change the Subject!

THINKING AND CHOOSING, ALFIE

Alfie came home from school crying and locked himself in his room. What happened, Alfie, I said? All his friends were mean to him and he had nobody to play with. Open the door, I said–I want to tell you a story.

Once there was a man who lived all by himself. One day, he found a magic box. When he opened it–a Genie appeared and showed him two islands. The one was full of people and the other was full of puppets. He could be King of either Island!

He saw all the problems on the People Island and he saw all the fun on the Puppet Island. The Puppets were dancing and dancing! Make me a Puppet, he said, I want to be King of the Puppets–I will call my Island–Utopia! His wish was granted.

As King of Puppet Island–he too danced and danced. No puppet disagreed with him or talked back. He was not unhappy–but he was not happy. In fact, he had no feeling at all. He was just like his subjects. There were no smiles, no kidding, no laughter, no cheers, no surprises, no tears of joy, no conversation, no kindness–no love. There was nothing! He didn't even get tired dancing–He was King Nothing and all his subjects were–objects!

If only he had chosen the People Island–why did he see only the problems?

We too, are sometime lonely, Alfie–especially when

people disappoint us. But you will be just like King Puppet if you try to hide in your room.

Someday, you will understand that the Creator couldn't make us puppets. We would be nothing! We must be able to think and choose to appreciate anything and be happy.

But the ability to think and choose can sometimes cause problems like your friends being mean to you. This was a decision for the Creator–giving man the ability to think and choose meant some men would choose right and some would choose wrong.

Once you think more about this, you can understand the need for reward and punishment. Parents and Courts reward and punish. Isn't there a need for this? The Parent and Judge are pleased to reward right, to show mercy and they both try to change those who do wrong. But what can they do if the person keeps doing wrong, doesn't care and is not sorry? Should the Parent who has six good children and one bad–not have had any–to prevent the bad?

Should the Creator–not have created?

But the Creator did create–and there are millions and millions of happy people–here and hereafter. For the Parent and Judge is–Our Father.

Well Alfie, at least you stopped crying. Tomorrow is another day and you will be playing again–Thinking and Choosing, Alfie.

THE BEST PLAN IS IN EFFECT, ALFIE

Last night, I was listening to the radio, Alfie, and it made me think of a number of things. I thought of the day I was driving home from work and a local station announced they were going to 'air' "Fiber McGee and Molly", that very night, at 7:30.

Great! I will gather all the kids in the living room and we can enjoy something together, using our imagination. It will be a lot of fun to watch their reaction instead of a picture on the tube. To share what you enjoy, with others, is a great way to spend an evening, I thought.

I was prepared. I knew nobody would be by the radio at 7:30—so, I made it an *order* and you were all there! However, I was so confident this was going to be the greatest half—hour you kids spent in a long time—that I gave my 'solemn word' you could leave anytime you wanted and I would not be mad!

Actually, I was glad you all left after a couple of minutes. I couldn't hear the program with all the noise you were making, anyway!

"If I ruled the world," the guy on the radio was singing. Sure, he could make everything 'peaches and cream'. He probably never had any kids!

Everything can be so perfect in a song. And usually, it is two people who don't need anybody else and are so happy just gazing at each other! I still like "Fiber McGee and Molly", or give me "Jack Benny" or "The Lone Ranger"!

But–what if I did rule the world? I could bring all those programs back and make everybody listen to them. I could pass out cigars–women and kids too–this is my world! But wait, maybe I am getting too selfish.

Of course–I would make everybody healthy and nobody would ever die. There would be no war–I would kill anybody who–not kill–but control anybody who didn't do what I wanted–well not necessarily what I wanted–but what the majority wanted–well at least half–well anyway, the ones who thought like me–since we know what is best whether they like it or not!

Now that I think about it, it wouldn't be any fun controlling things. Let somebody else do it. Why don't I leave it up to the guy singing?

But wait! The song shouldn't be "If I ruled the world", or even, if we ruled the world–how about–If They ruled the world?

They–the greatest song writers, the greatest intellectuals, all the Nobel prize winners, doctors, nurses, the father of the year, the movie stars–anybody and everybody–all the great thinkers and good people–what if they ruled the world? What a great place this would be!

Or–would they have some of my problems–as my little plan for the evening was ruined–would they, somehow, on this much larger scale lose control also? Maybe they couldn't make the people as good as them–maybe some of those in charge would not be as good as the rest and would take over! They could force me to listen to rock–noise!

Thank goodness! They're playing another song–I was getting carried away–Gee–I heard that song before–"He".

That's it! If He ruled the world, everything would be O.K.–that's what's needed–a Supreme Intellect!

Hold it–He tried too–and look at the result. People are sick and people do die. I heard a lady the other day yelling why me, Lord"–she listed all the things that were going wrong in her life–and then she was robbed! He let the robber get away–and He had all that lightning at His finger tips to stop him!

Then, I thought of the Puppet story, Alfie. And I remembered we need *free will* even with Somebody in control.

That lady had either identified the wrong person or yelled the wrong thing! She should have yelled "Why me, Robber", since the Lord didn't rob her–the robber did it all by himself with his own *free will*. Or, she should have yelled–"Why didn't you make him a puppet, Lord?" But wait–she couldn't yell since she would be a puppet too!

So, I thought, how could anybody but the Creator rule the world? Sure, there are a lot of questions we can't answer with our limited minds. But why do we need to know the answers?

I turned off the radio, Alfie, and looked out the window. I saw a lot of good–this world ain't so bad, I thought–I wouldn't change anything–I am satisfied to let somebody else control it. For, somehow I know what's happening is the best–no finite mind or minds are in control–the supreme Mind of the Creator is in control!

I think I will go to bed. My mind is tired out just pondering the magnificence of what's going on. Besides, everything is O.K.–The Best Plan Is In Effect, Alfie!

THIS TIME, THIS HOUR, ALFIE

Author's Note: The date this was written was not important. It was written on Thursday, the 12th of October, 1989–5 days prior to the tragedy on the S.F. bridge and highway, Tuesday, the 17th of October, 1989.

They were crossing the Bridge–four persons in all, two driving, two walking.

Mary had just gotten a new car. She would be the envy of the card party. Joan would be so angry–she will probably make an excuse and go home. I can't stand her, Mary thought. She waved to Paul, driving the other way in his Cadillac. What a woman, Paul thought. But he was too involved preparing his business speech. I will make more money than ever, he thought.

Swaying back and forth, was Frank. Frank didn't have a car. His wife took it when she left with the children. Frank didn't have a thought either. And if he did, he wouldn't remember it. He–'had a great time'–as he did every day now. No responsibility. Clutching to his six–pack, he mumbled to himself. He was no longer yelling–Frank was loud when he drank. He trudged slowly home to the only peace he knew–a long sleep.

Gerald was looking at the beautiful trees along the river–they had just reached their peak in brilliance. He looked over at Frank as they passed on opposite sides of the

Bridge. What an athlete Frank was, Gerald thought. He used to sway in the backfield when we were in high school, but not like that. If only I could have been an athlete like him. Why did my mother make me play the piano? Sure I am needed at get–togethers–when everybody wants to sing. But Frank is the life of the. . .

The Bridge collapsed!!

Two cars and four people–

Falling in Space!

Seconds and

Splash!

Poor Frank! Gerald thought, as he looked back from his swim to land. And the others? They knew not the time nor the hour.

Next week is my mother's birthday–I will play all her favorite songs, Gerald thought–as the tears welled in his eyes.

Alfie was still looking at the headline in the paper I had saved these so many years. I looked at him and wondered what his thoughts were–this time, this hour?

SUMDAY IS NOW, ALFIE!

One Sunday afternoon, Alfie and I were watching a movie and I fell asleep in the chair. Someday I will be a millionaire and then people will listen to me. I will have 490 million dollars!

Do you realize how much that is, Alfie, I said, when I awoke. That is 7 times 70! Alfie asked why I would need that much money? It was then that I really woke up. I think you're right, Alfie.

Many years ago there was a rich man who took all his possessions and stored them in a barn for someday. But that night he died. Was it too late for him, Alfie asked? I don't know. Sumday was then for him—but we can add up things today.

If we eliminate any wrong—we won't need to depend on 7 times 70 of forgiveness—we can store 7 x 70 of doing things for others—through prayer, actions, and just being nice to people. Today is the time, Alfie. Sumday is now!

ONE LINER AWAY, ALFIE

Ask and you shall receive–boomed the visiting priest! I think he scared himself. The mike in our church was as unpredictable as the babies attending the service. Now he is too low. What did he say? At least everybody is awake–prepared for another blast. In conclusion, he continued, ask not what you can do for God, ask what God can do for you.

Alfie remarked on the way home that he thought the priest made a mistake. He heard in school that a President once said "ask not what your Country can do for you, ask what you can do for your Country."

No Alfie, I said, Remember, the Creator is Our Father and we need His help for everything. Even to do something for Him, we need to ask for help. On our own we will fail. We must pray, the Our Father, the Rosary, and also in our own way.

Many years ago, men prayed to Christ–'Just say the word and he will be healed' 'I am not worthy' 'Have mercy on me a sinner' Remember me, when you come to your kingdom', 'Lord, that I may see'–and what was the response of Christ–immediate–you got it–as we say in our day.

Christ never said–don't bother me–pray for a few years–or anything like that–He said–'Go, he is cured' 'This day' 'Is there no one to condemn you'–'then neither do I'–and many other replies–one liners–as we call them. And there will be an immediate answer to our prayer, *in some way*, so pray the prayers we know–and pray in your own way–one liners to the Father and Christ.

You see Alfie, the Father can do things for us–even what seems impossible–but we don't need to tell Him how to answer our prayers–He knows how to do things. We can ask–but what we *need* is only a–One Liner Away, Alfie!

THE OMEGA, ALFIE

One early Sunday morning, while walking home from Church, it began to rain and soon the dry white sidewalk appeared to be slowly changing color as if there were a modern artist spraying from above. Alfie and I stopped under a tree.

It will soon be over, I assured him and with a sudden crack, a bolt of lightening struck, causing me to exclaim a heavenly remark! Alfie was unperturbed and asked–if that were closer–what is the kingdom of heaven like?

Well, Alfie, I said, the Omega is really the alpha. My eyes have never seen it and my ears have never heard what it is like and a man once said we could never imagine what it is like.

But years ago, there was a man on a tree who had not done much good and he was not about to have only a close call, like us. However, he saw no need for a question but rather made a request of the man on the tree next to him–to remember him when He came to His kingdom.

And you know Alfie, this man who never did much good should have been told to get lost–for what had he ever done for the man with the kingdom. It was the chance for this other man to tell him off–but He didn't, Alfie! He told him–that day he would be with Him in His kingdom!

The rain stopped and the sun began to shine as Alfie and I returned to the sidewalk. The Omega, Alfie, I said–is worth walking toward!

OUR FATHER, ALFIE

Over the years, Alfie, we have had many conversations and soon your big day will be here! I only have one more thing to tell you. I'll bet you thought I was finished yesterday when I spoke of the end, using the last word of the Greek alphabet, Omega.

Several times I have told you that you must be a child–that is–like a child. Christ himself, as man, referred to a Person, He called, Father, and told us to do the same. This makes us all children.

And this concept we can understand. Parents and Children. There have been many and many and many good parents over the years who love, and would do anything and have–for their children.

Would any of these dare to say that they were better than God? Then, if He is better than them–how much more will He do for His children!

The Creator who made children, necessarily knows all about his sons and daughters. He wants the best for them or he wouldn't be as good as an earthly parent!

Heaven then must be B.C.–Sawteg!

The end is the beginning. You cannot kill a spirit, only a body. The thinking part of you is separated. As said, in the burial Mass, "Life is changed, not taken away." To us, death is terrible and when one or many die, we are sad, and rightly so, for it is the end of something wonderful–this life.

But we must go on and live life without even thinking

of death or health–this will disturb Peace of Mind unless thoughts are directed toward the positive, Heaven.

Just be good and try the best you can, Alfie, that's all this earthly parent can ask. To use the statement, again, "Rise above the temptation to fear, to discouragement and to sadness, this distrust *paralyzes'* your activities. Be Serene! Be calm! and Joyous!" That's the way to live this life along with keeping the Commandments and loving people.

So–(back to Step, Alfie)–take one step at a time and never look back! It is a short distance to Heaven and everything is passing with each step! But what is needed, is Trust! Not fear!

Again, what Heaven is like, we don't know, for "the eye has not seen, nor has the ear heard, nor has it entered into the heart of man, what things God has prepared for those that do His will."

I guess that's it, Alfie, I wish I could tell you more but, as I said, I don't know what the beginning is like.

What's that, Alfie? Oh, what did I mean when I said, Heaven must be B.C.–Sawteg? Well, I was not trying to define Heaven–only my way of describing Heaven by using the first letter of the words–Heaven must be–Because of Christ–Stupendous, Awesome, Wonderful, Tremendous, Exciting–and God!

For, God is Supreme, He, the Creator, has all the power to make Heaven better than here and all the Love, to finally bring us–Total Peace and Happiness!

So, don't worry about anything, Alfie. He understands us–for–He is–Our Father, Alfie.

ME CRY, ALFIE?

Recently, a good friend gave me a book to read and .1 think everybody should read it—more than once. It made me laugh, think and choked me up. But I didn't cry, Alfie. "I'll Cry Tomorrow," as the movie said. But today, I am in control. No emotion for me!

But I think I do envy women who can cry. They can really enjoy a good movie. Brian's Song! I didn't cry then either.

But wait, Alfie—how can I tell you to be honest and tell you that. I watched that movie again by myself and I cried. That book didn't make me cry—maybe I will read it again.

Oh, I never told you the name of the book, "All I Really Need to Know I Learned in Kindergarten." (By Robert Fulghum).

And speaking of kindergarten, where did the years go? Tomorrow, Alfie, you will be the last of our four children to graduate. You are ready. You would be ready without me—but I like to think our little conversations helped.

And if I may quote Fulghum, "Who says people are no damn good? What kind of talk is that?"

And you will be another one of the 'good guys', Alfie. So, hold your head high and go forward—we're all on the same human team—and who cares about errors! As long as we play the game our best we win!

So, graduate Alfie and don't be afraid. Tomorrow is the day! Congratulations!

Me Cry, Alfie?

Breinigsville, PA USA
06 March 2011
256989BV00001BB/1/P